THE OFFICIAL

POKÉMON

ADVANCED®

Handbook #4

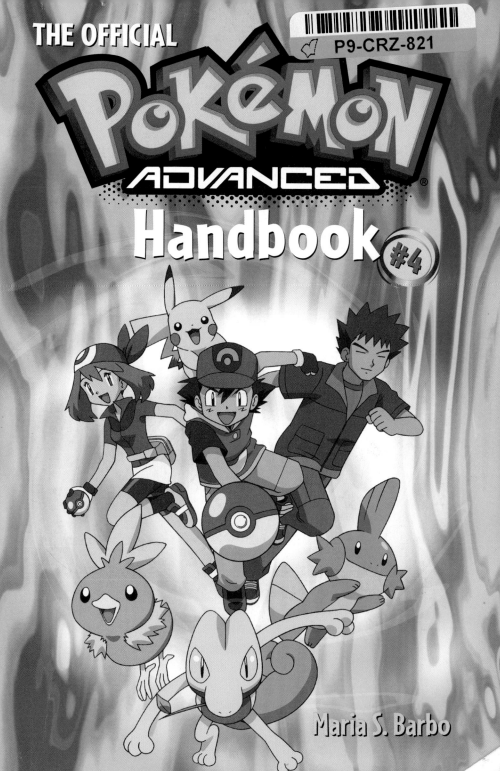

Maria S. Barbo

Scholastic Inc.

New York   Toronto   London   Auckland   Sydney
Mexico City   New Delhi   Hong Kong   Buenos Aires

ISBN: 0-439-55989-8

© 2003 Pokémon.
© 1995-2003 Nintendo/Creatures Inc./GAME FREAK inc.
TM & ® are trademarks of NIntendo.

Designed by Peter Koblish

12 11 10 9 8 7 6 5 4   3 4 5 6 7 8 9/0

Printed in the U.S.A.
First printing, October 2003

COMPETE! EXPLORE! DISCOVER! COLLECT!

Get ready for  **Pokémon** ADVANCED. This official Pokémon Handbook is your go-to guide for the complete info on a whole new world of Pokémon action and adventure.

CHECK THIS OUT!

🐾 Get the lowdown on more than 100 of the coolest, toughest, cutest, and newest Pokémon® Ruby and Pokémon® Sapphire characters!

🐾 Find out what's new, what's different, who's gone, and what's going on.

🐾 Say good-bye to some classic Pokémon and old friends.

🐾 Meet Ash's new friends . . . and his new foes.

🐾 Take a tour of the awesome Hoenn region.

🐾 Learn everything there is to know about the Pokémon League in Hoenn: how you start, what Pokémon you start with, where you go, and the new basics of Pokémon battle.

🐾 Flip to the master checklist at the back of the book. Use it to track your collection of Pokémon old and new.

POKéMON TRAINERS OF THE WORLD, ARE YOU READY?
THEN TURN THE PAGE AND PREPARE TO CATCH 'EM ALL!

WHAT'S NEW?

GET THIS PARTY STARTED

Pokémon trainers in Hoenn begin their journeys in Littleroot Town –
the town that stays true to its roots! And that's just the beginning. There's a whole new
world filled with brand-new Pokémon and Pokémon adventures!

WELCOME TO HOENN!

Ash Ketchum, his Pikachu, and all their friends are continuing their Pokémon journeys in Hoenn and so can you! With over a dozen towns, tons of places to visit, and lots to do, the Hoenn region is the place to be. You can dive to the bottom of the ocean and look for rare Pokémon in hidden caves or explore waterfalls, berry patches, lush forests, and sandy beaches. Hoenn has something for everyone!

TOP 5 COOLEST NEW THINGS ABOUT THE POKéMON LEAGUE
5. Contests and competitions
4. Hidden places packed with rare Pokémon
3. 2-on-2 battles
2. New friends!
1. More than 130 brand-new Pokémon!

TWO AT A TIME!

And we're not talking tag team. Hoenn makes its own rules, and here Pokémon battles are two-on-two. That means two of your Pokémon face off against two of your opponent's Pokémon . . . at the same time! The battle ends when one team of Pokémon is defeated. It's double the action and double the fun!

NEW ATTACKS!

Watch out, Pokémon trainers! The Pokémon in Hoenn know their stuff – and some new stuff too. New Pokémon Ruby and Pokémon Sapphire characters have new abilities – like Sharpedo's Rough Skin Attack. Even after Sharpedo swims away, its Rough Skin Attack continues to do damage to its opponent.

HAVE A BALL!

Pokémon technology is always advancing, and the Devon Corporation has created some brand-new Poké Balls like the Dive Ball, Nest Ball, Timer Ball, Luxury Ball, and Premier Ball to make it easier to catch those hard-to-capture Pokémon! Having a hard time adding Bug and Water-type Pokémon to your collection? Try using a Net Ball. Want to make it easier to catch a Pokémon you've already caught before? Invest in a Repeat Ball. There are so many Poké Balls to choose from!

NATURAL TALENTS

In addition to the moves your Pokémon use in battle, each Pokémon has its own special ability – like Synchronize, Shed Skin, or Pickup. You may have to tell your Pokémon what attacks to use in a face-off, but these special talents come naturally.

POKéMON WITH PERSONALITY

Did you know that a Pokémon's personality affects how it grows and develops? Your Pokémon might be bold, brave, or calm. Or your Pokémon may be quiet, lonely, and timid. An opponent may have one Pokémon who is jolly, and another that is serious. Personality makes every Pokémon unique!

BE A SHOW-OFF!

Want to show off your Pokémon's skills, talents, and good looks? Then take a rest stop in Hoenn. There are all kinds of contests trainers can join with their Pokémon. Your Pokémon will be judged on its toughness, cleverness, beauty, and even coolness! Each time your Pokémon enters and wins a contest, it gets ranked and wins awards!

EVOLUTIONS AND PREVOLUTIONS

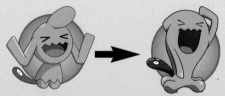

Some of your favorite Pokémon evolve into brand-new Pokémon. And some brand-new Pokémon evolve into your old favorites. Azurill is the pre-evolution of Marill and Wynaut is the pre-evolution of Wobbuffet. Check out the Pokédex pages in this book for the latest in evolution news!

TAKE A SIDE-QUEST

Hoenn is full of adventure. There's way more to do than just catch, battle, and train Pokémon. Take a break! Explore abandoned ships and caves, or build your own secret base. You can even discover hidden islands that only appear under top secret circumstances!

A LITTLE BIT OF LOVE

Some Pokémon will only evolve once they've learned to love and trust their trainers. Happy Pokémon spend a lot of time with their trainers, eat yummy healthy foods, and get daily workouts in Pokémon battles. And don't forget those regular check-ups at the Pokémon Center!

THAT'S SO LAST SEASON!

Did you know that some Pokémon are only around at certain times of the year? Pokémon like Surskit and Skitty are harder to find when they are out of season. How do you know if a Pokémon is in season? Watch the news on TV!

SKITTY   SURSKIT

GOT BERRIES?

Hoenn is filled with all different kinds of berry patches. Berries are nutritious and delicious – and Pokémon love to snack on them*. Berries, like the Cheri Berry, Chesto Berry, Pecha, Leppa, Oran, Sitrus, Wiki, Razz, Bluk, and Grepa Berry can give your Pokémon strength and energy! Did somebody say, "Yum?"

* Don't forget to replant the berries after your Pokémon have had their fill.

SOME THINGS NEVER CHANGE

Pokémon trainers in Hoenn still compete at Pokémon gyms to earn badges. They still collect and train a team of up to six Pokémon at one time. And they still get plenty of chances to explore, discover, compete, and collect!

HOW RANDOM!
Wurmple can evolve into either Silcoon or Cascoon depending on what time of day it evolves!

WURMPLE   SILCOON   CASCOON

IT'S ELEMENTAL!
Hoenn is filled with new Pokémon from the seventeen different elements: Normal, Fire, Water, Electric, Grass, Ice, Fighting, Poison, Ground, Flying, Psychic, Bug, Rock, Ghost, Dragon, Dark, and Steel.

NORMAL   FIRE   WATER   ICE

CASTFORM changes appearance depending upon the weather!

SCHOOL DAYS

Even Pokémon trainers have to go to school. Meet beginning trainers and learn facts about Pokémon at the Pokémon Trainers' School!

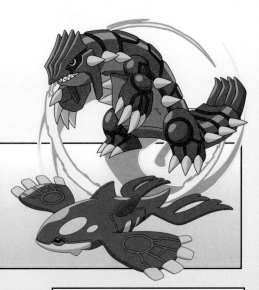

HOW RARE!

The bottom of Seafloor Cavern in the cave of Origin is the resting spot of two of the *rarest* Pokémon in Hoenn, Groudon, a Ground-type, and Kyogre, a Water-type.

DIVE!

In Hoenn, Pokémon like Relicanth, Clamperl, and Chinchou hide in the seaweed growing on the ocean floor. Now, you can search the ocean floor if you'd like to add some rare Pokémon to your team.

HIDE-AND-SEEK

In Hoenn, finding wild Pokémon might mean cutting down extra-tall grass, diving to the bottom of the ocean, surfing, and even smashing rocks!

UGLY FEEBAS

Feebas is an ugly Fish Pokémon that can evolve into the beautiful and tender, Milotic!

THE RUMOR MILL

People who live in Pacifidlog Town love gossip! One man tells of three legendary Pokémon made of ice, steel, and rock that live in Hoenn. Another tells the legend of a Pokémon who flies over Hoenn.

BE ON THE LOOK OUT!

Keep your ears open and your eyes up, and you might spot two new legendary Pokémon: Latios and Latias. According to an ancient legend, the two combination Dragon and Psychic Pokémon fly over the island of Altomare and protect it from evil.

NEW FRIENDS!

Brock rocks in his new clothes!

Meet May! May is ten years old and she's really interested in traveling and seeing new places! She never even threw a Poké Ball before she met Ash.

The first time May ever held a Poké Ball was when she used a Mudkip's Water Gun Attack to save Professor Birch from a pack of attacking Poochyena.

May's Torchic is the first Pokémon she's ever had! Torchic became fast friends with Ash's Pikachu!

Check out Ash's new outfit. Cool hat! When Ash journeys to Hoenn, he says good-bye to longtime Pokémon Bulbasaur and Charizard and starts fresh with Treecko and Mudkip.

Professor Birch gives new trainers their first Pokémon. He loves the great outdoors and likes to spend time out in the field working on experiments. And he loves, loves, *loves*, learning about all the new and rare Pokémon that can be found in the Hoenn region.

NO MORE MISTY!

Misty's taking a break from her Pokémon journey . . . and from Ash! She's back home in Cerulean City to head up the Pokémon gym with her sisters.

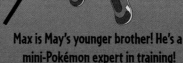

Max is May's younger brother! He's a mini-Pokémon expert in training!

NEW VILLAINS!

If you thought Team Rocket was bad, you ain't seen nothin' yet! Team Magma and Team Aqua are DOUBLE TROUBLE. Prepare for it! These dynamic duos are out to change the world — and not for the good.

TEAM AQUA

Team Aqua will trip you up with water-filled trenches. They raise sea levels to create more habitats for Water Pokémon . . . and they don't care who or what they wash out while they're at it!

TEAM MAGMA

Team Magma and their leader, Maxie, want to make more land for people and Pokémon. Too bad that means there won't be enough water. They'll throw lots of large land obstacles in your way.

Meowth and Wobbuffet still rock with Team Rocket!

Team Rocket's got a new Cacnea on its side. But will Cacnea's Grass Attacks be strong enough to catch the mighty Pikachu?

Team Rocket's Jessie and James will never give up on their ultimate quest to capture Pikachu!

BE AWARE. COMPARE.

How does Hoenn and the Pokémon League stack
up against the Indigo and Johto Leagues?
TAKE A LOOK:

	INDIGO LEAGUE	JOHTO LEAGUE	POKÉMON LEAGUE
Name of region :	Kanto	Johto	Hoenn
Number of badges to earn :	At least 8	At least 8	At least 8
Names of badges :	Cascade, Boulder, Soul, Rainbow, Earth, Marsh, Thunder, Volcano	Fog, Glacier, Mineral, Zephyr, Storm, Rising, Hive, Plain	Stone, Knuckle, Dynamo, Heat, Balance, Feather, Mind, Rain
Earning 8 badges qualifies Trainers to battle in :	The Pokémon League Tournament	The Johto League Championship	The Pokémon Championship
Gyms and Gym Leaders :	Brock (Pewter City)	Falkner (Violet City)	Roxanne (Rustboro City)
	Misty (Cerulean City)	Bugsy (Azalea Town)	Brawly (Dewford Town)
	Lt. Surge (Vermilion City)	Whitney (Goldenrod City)	Wattson (Mauville City)
	Erika (Celadon City)	Morty (Ecruteak City)	Flannery (Lavaridge Town)
	Janine (Fuchsia City)	Chuck (Cianwood City/Island)	Norman (Petalburg Gym)
	Sabrina (Saffron City)	Jasmine (Olivine City)	Winona (Fortree Gym)
	Blaine (Cinnabar Gym, but he's on the Seafoam Islands)	Pryce (Mahogany Town)	Tate and Liza (Mossdeep City)
	Gary (Viridian City)	Clair (Blackthorn City)	Wallace (Sootopolis City)

Trainers in the Indigo League begin their journeys in Pallet Town at the lab of Professor Oak. When it's time to pick their first Pokémon, their choices are:

| Bulbasaur | Charmander | Squirtle |
| Grass and Poison Type | Fire Type | Water Type |

Trainers who get their journeys started in New BarkTown belong to the Johto League. There, Professor Elm gives new trainers a choice between:

| Chikorita | Cyndaquil | Totodile |
| Grass Type | Fire Type | Water Type |

Trainers who join the Hoenn League rev their engines in Littleroot Town where Professor Birch keeps a stock of:

| Treecko | Torchic | Mudkip |
| Grass Type | Fire Type | Water Type |

SAY BUH-BYE!

Some of your favorite Pokémon are taking a break from all the competition. You won't see them in Hoenn and you won't see them in battle. But never fear, many of your favorite Pokémon from Pokémon Red and Blue and Pokémon Gold and Silver are still in action. You'll find a complete list of all the Pokémon in Hoenn at the back of this book. Here are a few of your favorites who are sticking around:

Abra™ Alakazam™ Azumarill™ Bellossom™ Chinchou™

Corsola™ Crobat™ Dodrio™ Doduo™ Donphan™

Electrode™ Geodude™ Girafarig™ Gloom™ Golbat™

Goldeen™ Golduck™ Golem™ Graveler™ Grimer™

Gyarados™ Heracross™ Horsea™ Igglybuff™ Jigglypuff™

Kadabra™ Kingdra™ Koffing™ Lanturn™ Machamp™

Machoke™   Machop™   Magcargo™   Magikarp™   Magnemite™

Magneton™   Marill™   Muk™   Natu™   Ninetails™

Oddish™   Phanpy™   Pichu™   Pikachu™   Pinsir™

Psyduck™   Raichu™   Rhydon™   Rhyhorn™   Sandshrew™

Sandslash™   Seadra™   Seaking™   Skarmony™   Slugma™   Starmie™

Staryu™   Tentacool™   Tentacruel™   Vileplume™   Voltorb™

Vulpix™   Weezing™   Wigglytuff™   Wobbuffet™   Xatu™   Zubat™

POKéMON HALL OF FAME

Whoa! Ash, May, and Pikachu discover a Relicanth in a secret cave.

May's Torchic uses Fire Spin to escape Mudkip's wet and wild Water Gun Attack!

Ash's first meeting with May wipes him out!

Vigoroth is in an uproar! Pikachu, Thundershock now! Watch out for those Fury Swipes!

Pikachu shocks Taillow with an electrifying Thundershock!

Can Treecko save Pikachu from Team Rocket's attacking Cacnea?

SUPER-CHARGE YOUR POKéDEX!

Professor Birch knows everything there is to know about the Pokémon in Hoenn. And lucky for you, he's programmed all the info into this brand-new, upgraded Pokédex.

NOW GET READY TO LEARN EVERYTHING THERE IS TO KNOW ABOUT ALL THE BRAND-NEW POKéMON!

TREECKO
Wood Gecko Pokémon
TYPE: Grass
HEIGHT: 1' 8"
WEIGHT: 11 lbs.
ATTACKS: Pound, Leer, Absorb, Quick Attack, Pursuit, Screech, Mega Drain, Agility, Slam, Detect, Giga Drain

GROVYLE
Wood Gecko Pokémon
TYPE: Grass
HEIGHT: 2' 11"
WEIGHT: 45 lbs.
ATTACKS: Pound, Leer, Absorb, Quick Attack, Fury Cutter, Pursuit, Screech, Leaf Blade, Agility, Slam, Detect, False Swipe

SCEPTILE
Forest Pokémon
TYPE: Grass
HEIGHT: 5' 7"
WEIGHT: 115 lbs.
ATTACKS: Pound, Leer, Absorb, Quick Attack, Fury Cutter, Pursuit, Screech, Leaf Blade, Agility, Slam, Detect, False Swipe

 →  →

TORCHIC
Chick Pokémon
TYPE: Fire
HEIGHT: 1' 4"
WEIGHT: 6 lbs.
ATTACKS: Poison Sting, Supersonic, Constrict, Acid, Bubblebeam, Wrap, Barrier, Screech, Hydro Pump

COMBUSKEN
Young Fowl Pokémon
TYPE: Fire/Fighting
HEIGHT: 2' 11"
WEIGHT: 43 lbs.
ATTACKS: Scratch, Growl, Focus Energy, Ember, Double Kick, Peck, Sand Attack, Slash, Mirror Move, Sky Uppercut

BLAZIKEN
Blaze Pokémon
TYPE: Fire/Fighting
HEIGHT: 6' 3"
WEIGHT: 115 lbs.
ATTACKS: Fire Punch, Scratch, Growl, Focus Energy, Ember, Double Kick, Peck, Sand Attack, Bulk Up, Quick Attack, Blaze Kick, Slash, Mirror Move, Sky Uppercut

MUDKIP
Mud Fish Pokémon
TYPE: Water
HEIGHT: 1' 4"
WEIGHT: 17 lbs.
ATTACKS: Tackle, Growl, Mud-Slap, Water Gun, Bide, Foresight, Mud Sport, Take Down, Whirlpool, Protect, Hydro Pump, Endeavor

MARSHTOMP
Mud Fish Pokémon
TYPE: Water/Ground
HEIGHT: 2' 4"
WEIGHT: 62 lbs.
ATTACKS: Tackle, Growl, Mud-Slap, Water Gun, Bide, Mud Shot, Foresight, Mud Sport, Take Down, Muddy Water, Protect, Earthquake

SWAMPERT
Mud Fish Pokémon
TYPE: Water/Ground
HEIGHT: 4' 11"
WEIGHT: 181 lbs.
ATTACKS: Tackle, Growl, Mud-Slap, Water Gun, Bide, Mud Shot, Foresight, Mud Sport, Take Down, Muddy Water, Protect, Earthquake, Endeavor

POOCHYENA
Bite Pokémon
TYPE: Dark
HEIGHT: 1' 8"
WEIGHT: 30 lbs.
ATTACKS: Tackle, Howl, Sand Attack, Bite, Odor Sleuth, Roar, Swagger, Scary Face, Take Down, Taunt, Crunch, Thief

MIGHTYENA
Bite Pokémon
TYPE: Dark
HEIGHT: 3' 3"
WEIGHT: 82 lbs.
ATTACKS: Tackle, Howl, Sand Attack, Howl, Odor Sleuth, Roar, Swagger, Scary Face, Take Down, Taunt, Crunch, Thief

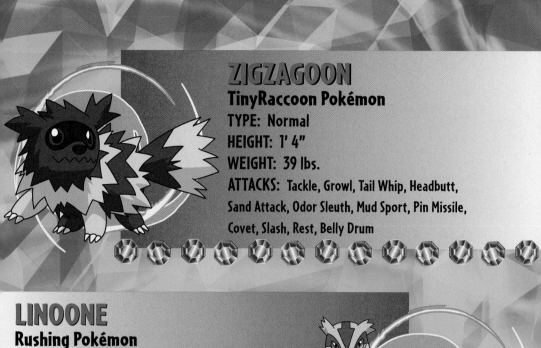

ZIGZAGOON
TinyRaccoon Pokémon
TYPE: Normal
HEIGHT: 1' 4"
WEIGHT: 39 lbs.
ATTACKS: Tackle, Growl, Tail Whip, Headbutt,
Sand Attack, Odor Sleuth, Mud Sport, Pin Missile,
Covet, Slash, Rest, Belly Drum

LINOONE
Rushing Pokémon
TYPE: Normal
HEIGHT: 1' 8"
WEIGHT: 72 lbs.
ATTACKS: Rushing, Tackle, Growl, Tail Whip, Headbutt,
Sand Attack, Odor Sleuth, Mud Sport, Fury Swipes, Covet, Slash,
Rest, Belly Drum

WURMPLE **Worm Pokémon**
TYPE: Bug • **HEIGHT:** 1' 0" • **WEIGHT:** 8 lbs.
ATTACKS: Tackle, String Shot, Poison Sting

SILCOON **Cocoon Pokémon**
TYPE: Bug • **HEIGHT:** 2' 0" • **WEIGHT:** 22 lbs.
ATTACKS: Harden

BEAUTIFLY **Butterfly Pokémon**
TYPE: Bug/Flying • **HEIGHT:** 3' 3" • **WEIGHT:** 63 lbs.
ATTACKS: Absorb, Gust, Stun Spore, Mornin, Mega Drain, Giga Drain

CASCOON **Cocoon Pokémon**
TYPE: Bug • **HEIGHT:** 2' 4" • **WEIGHT:** 43 lbs.
ATTACKS: Harden

DUSTOX **Toxic Moth Pokémon**
TYPE: Bug/Poison • **HEIGHT:** 3' 11" • **WEIGHT:** 70 lbs.
ATTACKS: Confusion, Gust, Protect, Moonlight, Psybeam, Light Screen, Toxic

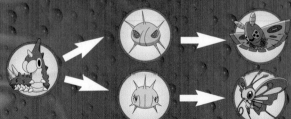

LOTAD
Water Weed Pokémon
TYPE: Water/Grass
HEIGHT: 1' 8"
WEIGHT: 61 lbs.
ATTACKS: Astonish, Growl, Absorb, Nature Power, Mist, Rain Dance, Mega Drain

LOMBRE
Jolly Pokémon
TYPE: Water/Grass
HEIGHT: 3' 11"
WEIGHT: 72 lbs.
ATTACKS: Astonish, Growl, Absorb, Nature Power, Fake Out, Fury Swipes, Water Sport, Thief, Uproar, Hydro Pump

LUDICOLO
Carefree Pokémon
TYPE: Water/Grass
HEIGHT: 4' 11"
WEIGHT: 121 lbs.
ATTACKS: Astonish, Growl, Absorb, Nature Power

SEEDOT

Acorn Pokémon

TYPE: Grass

HEIGHT: 1' 8"

WEIGHT: 9 lbs.

ATTACKS: Bide, Harden, Growth, Nature Power, Synthesis, Sunny Day, Explosion

NUZLEAF

Wily Pokémon

TYPE: Grass/Dark

HEIGHT: 3' 3"

WEIGHT: 62 lbs.

ATTACKS: Pound, Harden, Growth, Nature Power, Fake Out, Torment, Faint, Razor Wind, Swagger, Extrasensory

SHIFTRY

Wicked Pokémon

TYPE: Grass/Dark

HEIGHT: 4' 3"

WEIGHT: 131 lbs.

ATTACKS: Pound, Harden, Growth, Nature Power

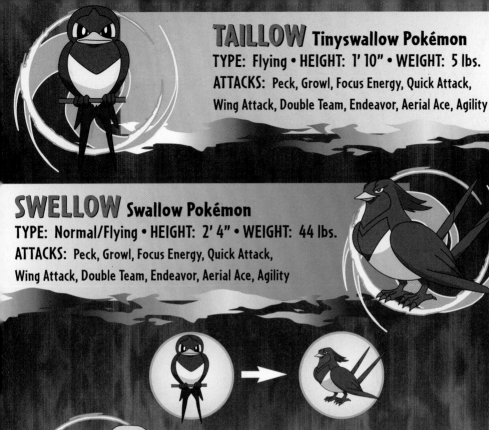

TAILLOW Tinyswallow Pokémon

TYPE: Flying • HEIGHT: 1' 10" • WEIGHT: 5 lbs.

ATTACKS: Peck, Growl, Focus Energy, Quick Attack, Wing Attack, Double Team, Endeavor, Aerial Ace, Agility

SWELLOW Swallow Pokémon

TYPE: Normal/Flying • HEIGHT: 2' 4" • WEIGHT: 44 lbs.

ATTACKS: Peck, Growl, Focus Energy, Quick Attack, Wing Attack, Double Team, Endeavor, Aerial Ace, Agility

WINGULL Seagull Pokémon

TYPE: Water/Flying • HEIGHT: 2' 0" • WEIGHT: 211 lbs.

ATTACKS: Growl, Water Gun, Supersonic, Wing Attack, Mist, Quick Attack, Pursuit, Agility

PELIPPER Water Bird Pokémon

TYPE: Normal/Flying • HEIGHT: 2' 11" • WEIGHT: 43 lbs.

ATTACKS: Growl, Water Gun, Water Sport, Wing Attack, Supersonic, Mist, Protect, Stockpile, Swallow, Spit Up, Hydro Pump

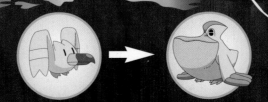

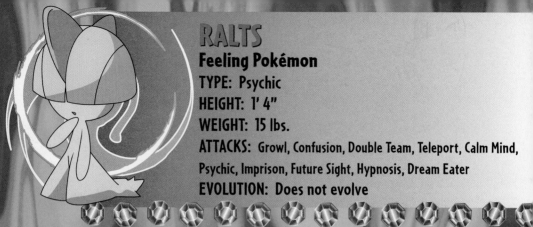

RALTS

Feeling Pokémon

TYPE: Psychic

HEIGHT: 1' 4"

WEIGHT: 15 lbs.

ATTACKS: Growl, Confusion, Double Team, Teleport, Calm Mind, Psychic, Imprison, Future Sight, Hypnosis, Dream Eater

EVOLUTION: Does not evolve

KIRLIA

Emotion Pokémon

TYPE: Psychic

HEIGHT: 2' 7"

WEIGHT: 45 lbs.

ATTACKS: Growl, Confusion, Double Team, Teleport, Calm Mind, Psychic, Imprison, Future Sight, Hypnosis, Dream Eater

GARDEVOIR

Embrace Pokémon

TYPE: Psychic

HEIGHT: 5' 3"

WEIGHT: 107 lbs.

ATTACKS: Growl, Confusion, Double Team, Teleport, Calm Mind, Psychic, Imprison, Future Sight, Hypnosis, Dream Eater

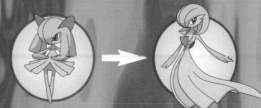

SURSKIT Pond Skater Pokémon

TYPE: Bug/Water • HEIGHT: 1' 8" • WEIGHT: 4 lbs.

ATTACKS: Bubble Quick, Sweet Scent, Water Sport, Bubblebeam, Agility, Mist, Haze

MASQUERAIN Eyeball Pokémon

TYPE: Bug/Flying • HEIGHT: 2' 7" • WEIGHT: 8 lbs.

ATTACKS: Bubble Quick, Sweet Scent, Water Sport, Gust, Scary Face, Stun Spore, Silver Wind, Whirlwind

SHROOMISH Mushroom Pokémon

TYPE: Grass • HEIGHT: 1' 4" • WEIGHT: 10 lbs.

ATTACKS: Absorb, Tackle, Stun Spore, Leech Seed, Mega Drain, Headbutt, Poison Powder, Growth, Giga Drain, Spore

BRELOOM Mushroom Pokémon

TYPE: Grass/Fighting • HEIGHT: 3' 11" • WEIGHT: 86 lbs.

ATTACKS: Absorb, Tackle, Stun Spore, Leech Seed, Mega Drain, Headbutt, Mach Punch, Counter, Sky Uppercut, Mind Reader, Dynamicpunch

SLAKOTH
Slacker Pokémon
TYPE: Normal
HEIGHT: 2' 7"
WEIGHT: 53 lbs.
ATTACKS: Scratch, Yawn, Encore, Slack Off,
Faint Attack, Amnesia, Covet, Counter, Flail

VIGOROTH
Wild Monkey Pokémon
TYPE: Normal
HEIGHT: 4' 7"
WEIGHT: 103 lbs.
ATTACKS: Scratch, Focus Energy, Encore, Uproar,
Fury Swipes, Endure, Slash, Counter, Focus Punch, Reversal

SLAKING
Lazy Pokémon
TYPE: Normal
HEIGHT: 6' 7"
WEIGHT: 288 lbs.
ATTACKS: Scratch, Yawn, Encore, Slack off, Faint, Amnesia, Covet,
Swagger, Counter, Flail

NINCADA

Trainee Pokémon

TYPE: Psychic

HEIGHT: 1' 8"

WEIGHT: 12lbs.

ATTACKS: Scratch, Harden, Leech Life, Sand Attack, Fury Swipes, Mind Reader, False Swipe, Mud-Slap, Metal Claw, Dig

NINJASK

Ninja Pokémon

TYPE: Bug/Flying

HEIGHT: 2' 7"

WEIGHT: 26 lbs

ATTACKS: Scratch, Harden, Leech Life, Sand Attack, Fury Swipes, Mind Reader, Double Team, Fury Cutter, Screech, Swords Dance, Slash, Agility, Baton Pass

SHEDINJA

Shed Pokémon

TYPE: Bug/Ghost

HEIGHT: 2' 7"

WEIGHT: 3 lbs.

ATTACKS: Scratch, Harden, Leech Life, Sand Attack, Fury Swipes, Mind Reader, Spite, Confuse Ray, Shadow Ball, Grudge

WHISMUR

Whisper Pokémon

TYPE: Normal

HEIGHT: 2'

WEIGHT: 36 lbs.

ATTACKS: Pound, Uproar, Astonish, Howl, Supersonic, Stomp, Screech, Roar, Rest, Sleep Talk, Hyper Voice

LOUDRED

Big Voice Pokémon

TYPE: Normal

HEIGHT: 3' 3"

WEIGHT: 89 lbs.

ATTACKS: Pound, Uproar, Astonish, Howl, Supersonic, Stomp, Screech, Roar, Rest, Sleep Talk, Hyper Voice

EXPLOUD

Loud Noise Pokémon

TYPE: Normal

HEIGHT: 4' 11"

WEIGHT: 185 lbs.

ATTACKS: Pound, Uproar, Astonish, Howl, Supersonic, Stomp, Screech, Hyper Beam, Roar, Rest, Sleep Talk, Hyper Voice

MAKUHITA Guts Pokémon
TYPE: Fighting • HEIGHT: 3' 3" WEIGHT: 191 lbs.
ATTACKS: Tackle, Focus, Energy, Sand Attack, Arm Thrust, Vital
Throw, Fake Out, Whirlwind, Knock Off, Smellingsalt, Belly Drum,
Endure, Seismic Toss, Reversal

HARIYAMA Arm Thrust Pokémon
TYPE: Fighting • HEIGHT: 7' 7" • WEIGHT: 560 lbs.
ATTACKS: Tackle, Focus, Energy, Sand Attack, Arm Thrust,
Vital Throw, Fake Out, Knock Off, Smellingsalt, Belly Drum,
Endure, Seismic Toss, Reversal

AZURILL
Polka Dot Pokémon
TYPE: Normal
HEIGHT: 8"
WEIGHT: 4 lbs.
ATTACKS: Splash, Charm, Tail Whip, Bubble, Slam, Water Gun

NOSEPASS
Compass Pokémon
TYPE: Rock
HEIGHT: 3' 3"
WEIGHT: 214 lbs.
ATTACKS: Tackle, Harden, Rock Throw, Block, Thunder
Wave, Rock Slide, Sandstorm, Rest, Zap Cannon, Lock-On
EVOLUTION: Does not evolve

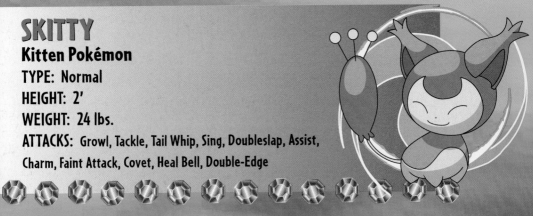

SKITTY
Kitten Pokémon
TYPE: Normal
HEIGHT: 2'
WEIGHT: 24 lbs.
ATTACKS: Growl, Tackle, Tail Whip, Sing, Doubleslap, Assist,
Charm, Faint Attack, Covet, Heal Bell, Double-Edge

DELCATTY
Prim Pokémon
TYPE: Normal
HEIGHT: 3' 7"
WEIGHT: 72 lbs.
ATTACKS: Growl, Sing, Doubleslap

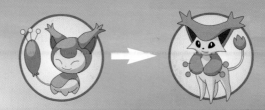

SABLEYE
Darkness Pokémon
TYPE: Dark/Ghost
HEIGHT: 1' 8"
WEIGHT: 24 lbs.
ATTACKS: Leer, Scratch, Foresight, Night Shade, Astonish, Fury Swipes, Fake Out, Detect, Faint Attack, Knock Off, Confuse Ray, Shadow Ball, Mean Look
EVOLUTION: Does not evolve

MAWILE
Deceiver Pokémon
TYPE: Steel
HEIGHT: 2' 0"
WEIGHT: 25 lbs.
ATTACKS: Astonish, Fake Tears, Bite, Sweet Scent, Vicegrip, Faint Attack, Baton Pass, Crunch, Iron Defense, Stockpile, Swallow, Spit Up
EVOLUTION: Does not evolve

ARON

Iron Armor Pokémon

TYPE: Steel/Rock

HEIGHT: 1' 4"

WEIGHT: 132 lbs.

ATTACKS: Tackle, Harden, Mud-Slap, Headbutt, Metal Claw, Iron Defense, Roar, Take Down, Iron Tail, Protect, Metal Sound, Double-Edge

LAIRON

Iron Armor Pokémon

TYPE: Steel/Rock

HEIGHT: 2' 11"

WEIGHT: 265 lbs.

ATTACKS: Tackle, Harden, Mud-Slap, Headbutt, Metal Claw, Iron Defense, Roar, Take Down, Iron Tail, Protect, Metal Sound, Double-Edge

AGGRON

Iron Armor Pokémon

TYPE: Steel/Rock

HEIGHT: 6' 11"

WEIGHT: 794 lbs.

ATTACKS: Tackle, Harden, Mud-Slap, Headbutt, Metal Claw, Iron Defense, Roar, Take Down, Iron Tail, Protect, Metal Sound, Double-Edge

MEDITITE
Meditate Pokémon
TYPE: Fighting/Psychic
HEIGHT: 2' 0"
WEIGHT: 25 lbs.
ATTACKS: Bide, Meditate, Confusion, Detect, Hidden Power, Mind Reader, Clam Mind, Hi Jump Kick, Psych Up, Reversal, Recover

MEDICHARM
Meditate Pokémon
TYPE: Fighting/Psychic
HEIGHT: 4' 3"
WEIGHT: 69 lbs.
ATTACKS: Fire Punch, Thunderpunch, Ice Punch, Bide, Meditate, Confusion, Detect, Hidden Power, Mind Reader, Calm Mind, Hi Jump Kick, Psych Up, Reversal, Recover

ELECTRIKE
Lightning Pokémon
TYPE: Electric
HEIGHT: 2' 0"
WEIGHT: 34 lbs.
ATTACKS: Tackle, Thunder Wave, Leer, Howl, Quick, Spark, Odor Sleuth, Roar, Bite, Thunder, Charge

MANECTRIC
Discharge Pokémon
TYPE: Electric
HEIGHT: 4' 11"
WEIGHT: 89 lbs.
ATTACKS: Tackle, Thunder Wave, Leer, Howl, Quick, Spark, Odor Sleuth, Roar, Bite, Thunder, Charge

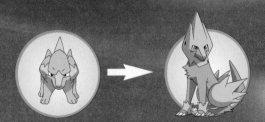

PLUSLE

Cheering Pokémon

TYPE: Electric

HEIGHT: 1' 4"

WEIGHT: 9 lbs.

ATTACKS: Growl, Thunder Wave, Quick, Helping Hand, Spark, Encore, Fake Tears, Charge, Thunder, Baton Pass, Agility

EVOLUTION: Does not evolve

MINUN

Cheering Pokémon

TYPE: Electric

HEIGHT: 1' 4"

WEIGHT: 9 lbs.

ATTACKS: Growl, Thunder Wave, Quick, Helping Hand, Spark, Encore, Charm, Charge, Thunder, Baton Pass, Agility

EVOLUTION: Does not evolve

VOLBEAT
Firefly Pokémon
TYPE: Bug
HEIGHT: 2' 4"
WEIGHT: 39 lbs.
ATTACKS: Tackle, Confuse Ray, Double Team, Moonlight, Quick Attack, Wish, Encore, Flatter, Helping Hand, Covet
EVOLUTION: Does not evolve

ILLUMISE
Firefly Pokémon
TYPE: Bug
HEIGHT: 2' 0"
WEIGHT: 39 lbs.
ATTACKS: Tackle, Sweet Scent, Charm, Moonlight, Quick, Wish, Encore, Flatter, Helping Hand, Covet
EVOLUTION: Does not evolve

ROSELIA
Thorn Pokémon
TYPE: Grass/Poison
HEIGHT: 1' 0"
WEIGHT: 4 lbs.
ATTACKS: Absorb, Growth, Poison Sting, Stun Spore, Mega Drain, Leech Seed, Magical Leaf, Grasswhistle, Giga Drain, Sweet Scent, Ingrain, Toxic, Petal Dance, Aroma Therapy, Synthesis
EVOLUTION: Does not evolve

GULPIN
Stomach Pokémon
TYPE: Poison
HEIGHT: 1' 4"
WEIGHT: 23 lbs.
ATTACKS: Pound, Yawn, Poison Gas, Sludge, Amnesia, Encore, Toxic, Stockpile, Spit Up, Swallow, Sludge Bomb

SWALOT
Poison Bag Pokémon
TYPE: Poison
HEIGHT: 5' 7"
WEIGHT: 176 lbs.
ATTACKS: Pound, Yawn, Poison Gas, Sludge, Amnesia, Encore, Body Slam, Toxic, Stockpile, Spit Up, Swallow, Sludge Bomb

CARVANHA
Savage Pokémon
TYPE: Water/Dark
HEIGHT: 2' 7"
WEIGHT: 46 lbs.
ATTACKS: Leer, Bite, Rage, Focus Energy, Scary Face, Crunch, Screech, Take Down, Swagger, Agility

SHARPEDO
Brutal Pokémon
TYPE: Water/Dark
HEIGHT: 5' 11"
WEIGHT: 196 lbs.
ATTACKS: Leer, Bite, Rage, Focus Energy, Scary Face, Crunch, Screech, Slash, Taunt, Swagger, Skull Bash, Agility

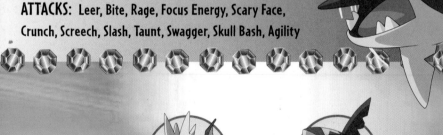

WAILMER

Ball Whale Pokémon

TYPE: Water

HEIGHT: 6' 7"

WEIGHT: 287 lbs.

ATTACKS: Splash, Growl, Water Gun, Rollout, Whirlpool, Astonish, Water Pulse, Mist, Rest, Water Spout, Amnesia, Hydro Pump

WAILORD

Float Whale Pokémon

TYPE: Water

HEIGHT: 47' 7"

WEIGHT: 878 lbs.

ATTACKS: Splash, Growl, Water Gun, Rollout, Whirlpool, Astonish, Water Pulse, Mist, Rest, Water Spout, Amnesia, Hydro Pump

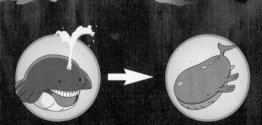

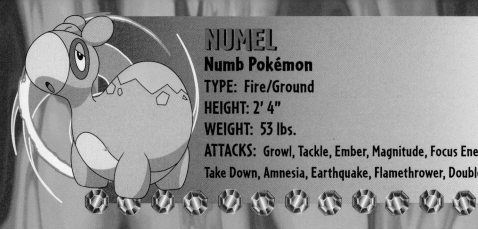

NUMEL
Numb Pokémon
TYPE: Fire/Ground
HEIGHT: 2' 4"
WEIGHT: 53 lbs.
ATTACKS: Growl, Tackle, Ember, Magnitude, Focus Energy, Take Down, Amnesia, Earthquake, Flamethrower, Double-Edge

CAMERUPT
Eruption Pokémon
TYPE: Fire/Ground
HEIGHT: 6' 3"
WEIGHT: 485 lbs.
ATTACKS: Growl, Tackle, Ember, Magnitude, Focus Energy, Take Down, Amnesia, Rock Slide, Earthquake, Eruption, Fissure

TORKOAL
Coal Pokémon
TYPE: Fire
HEIGHT: 1' 8"
WEIGHT: 177 lbs.
ATTACKS: Ember, Smog, Curse, Smokescreen, Fire Spin, Body Slam, Protect, Flamethrower, Iron Defense, Amnesia, Flail, Heat Wave
EVOLUTION: Does not evolve

SPOINK
Bounce Pokémon
TYPE: Psychic
HEIGHT: 2' 4"
WEIGHT: 67 lbs.
ATTACKS: Splash, Psywave, Odor Sleuth, Fsybeam, Psych Up, Confuse, Ray, Magic Coat, Psychic, Rest, Snore, Bounce

GRUMPIG
Manipulate Pokémon
TYPE: Psychic
HEIGHT: 2' 11"
WEIGHT: 158 lbs.
ATTACKS: Splash, Psywave, Odor Sleuth, Psybeam, Spywave, Psych Up, Confuse Ray, Magic Coat, Psychic, Rest, Snore, Bounce

SPINDA
Spot Panda Pokémon
TYPE: Normal
HEIGHT: 3' 7"
WEIGHT: 11 lbs.
ATTACKS: Tackle, Uproar, Faint, Psybeam, Hypnosis, Dizzy Punch, Teeter Dance, Psych Up, Double-Edge, Flail, Thrash
EVOLUTION: Does not evolve

TRAPINCH
Ant Pit Pokémon
TYPE: Ground
HEIGHT: 2' 4"
WEIGHT: 33 lbs.
ATTACKS: Bite, Sand, Faint, Sand Tomb, Crunch, Dig, Sandstorm, Hyper Beam
EVOLUTION: Does not evolve

VIBRAVA
Vibration Pokémon
TYPE: Ground/Dragon
HEIGHT: 3' 7"
WEIGHT: 34 lbs
ATTACKS: Bite, Sand, Faint, Sand Tomb, Crunch, Dragonbreath, Screech, Sandstorm, Hyper Beam

FLYGON
Mystic Pokémon
TYPE: Ground/Dragon
HEIGHT: 3' 7"
WEIGHT: 181 lbs.
ATTACKS: Bite, Sand, Faint, Sand Tomb, Crunch, Dragonbreath, Screech, Sandstorm, Hyper Beam

CACNEA
Cactus Pokémon
TYPE: Grass
HEIGHT: 1' 4"
WEIGHT: 113 lbs.
ATTACKS: Poison Sting, Leer, Absorb, Growth, Leech Seed, Sand, Pin Missile, Ingrain, Faint, Spikes, Needle Arm, Cotton Spore, Sandstorm

CACTURNE
Scarecrow Pokémon
TYPE: Grass/Dark
HEIGHT: 4' 3"
WEIGHT: 171 lbs.
ATTACKS: Poison Sting, Leer, Absorb, Growth, Leech Seed, Sand, Pin Missile, Ingrain, Faint, Spikes, Needle Arm, Cotton Spore, Sandstorm

SWABLU

Cotton Bird Pokémon

TYPE: Normal/Flying

HEIGHT: 1' 4"

WEIGHT: 3 lbs.

ATTACKS: Peck Growl, Astonish, Sing, Fury, Safeguard, Mist, Take Down, Mirror Move, Refresh, Perish Song

ALTARIA

Humming Pokémon

TYPE: Dragon/Flying

HEIGHT: 3' 7"

WEIGHT: 45 lbs.

ATTACKS: Peck Growl, Astonish, Sing, Fury, Safeguard, Mist, Take Down, Dragonbreath, Dragon Dance, Refresh, Perish Song

ZANGOOSE
Cat Ferret Pokémon
TYPE: Normal
HEIGHT: 4' 3"
WEIGHT: 89 lbs.
ATTACKS: Scratch, Leer, Quick, Swords Dance, Fury Cutter, Slash, Pursuit, Crush Claw, Taunt, Detect, False Swipe
EVOLUTION: Does not evolve

SEVIPER
Fang Snake Pokémon
TYPE: Poison
HEIGHT: 8' 10"
WEIGHT: 116 lbs.
ATTACKS: Wrap, Lick, Bite, Poison Tail, Screech, Glare, Crunch, Poison Fang, Swagger, Haze
EVOLUTION: Does not evolve

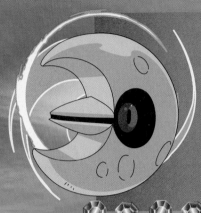

LUNATONE
Meteorite Pokémon
TYPE: Rock/Psychic
HEIGHT: 3' 3"
WEIGHT: 370 lbs.
ATTACKS: Tackle, Harden, Confusion, Rock Throw, Hypnosis, Psywave, Cosmic Power, Psychic, Future Sight, Explosion
EVOLUTION: Does not evolve

SOLROCK
Meteorite Pokémon
TYPE: Rock/Psychic
HEIGHT: 3' 11"
WEIGHT: 340 lbs.
ATTACKS: Tackle, Harden, Confusion, Rock Throw, Fire Spin, Psywave, Cosmic Power, Rock Slide, Solarbeam, Explosion
EVOLUTION: Does not evolve

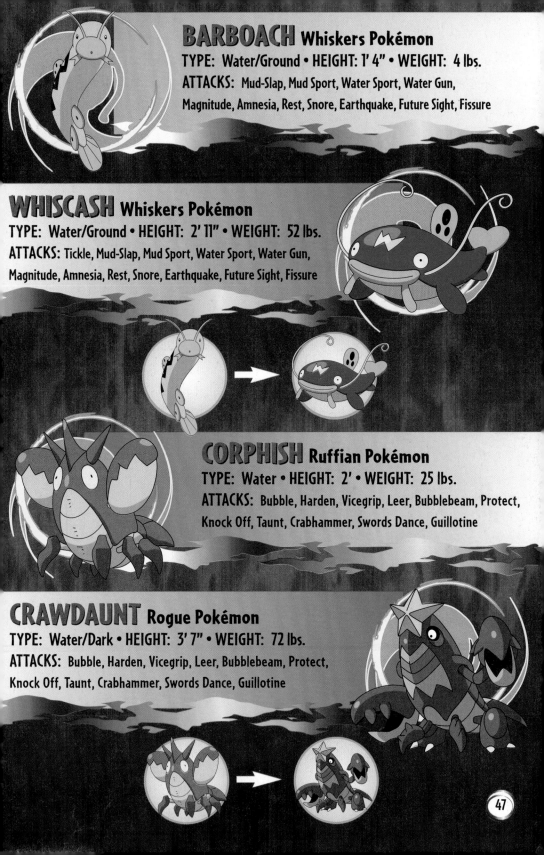

BARBOACH Whiskers Pokémon

TYPE: Water/Ground • HEIGHT: 1' 4" • WEIGHT: 4 lbs.

ATTACKS: Mud-Slap, Mud Sport, Water Sport, Water Gun, Magnitude, Amnesia, Rest, Snore, Earthquake, Future Sight, Fissure

WHISCASH Whiskers Pokémon

TYPE: Water/Ground • HEIGHT: 2' 11" • WEIGHT: 52 lbs.

ATTACKS: Tickle, Mud-Slap, Mud Sport, Water Sport, Water Gun, Magnitude, Amnesia, Rest, Snore, Earthquake, Future Sight, Fissure

CORPHISH Ruffian Pokémon

TYPE: Water • HEIGHT: 2' • WEIGHT: 25 lbs.

ATTACKS: Bubble, Harden, Vicegrip, Leer, Bubblebeam, Protect, Knock Off, Taunt, Crabhammer, Swords Dance, Guillotine

CRAWDAUNT Rogue Pokémon

TYPE: Water/Dark • HEIGHT: 3' 7" • WEIGHT: 72 lbs.

ATTACKS: Bubble, Harden, Vicegrip, Leer, Bubblebeam, Protect, Knock Off, Taunt, Crabhammer, Swords Dance, Guillotine

BALTOY Clay Doll Pokémon

TYPE: Ground/Psychic • **HEIGHT:** 1' 8" • **WEIGHT:** 47 lbs.
ATTACKS: Confusion, Harden, Rapid Spin, Mud-Slap, Psybeam, Rock Tomb, Self-Destruct, Ancientpower, Sandstorm

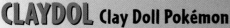

CLAYDOL Clay Doll Pokémon

TYPE: Ground/Psychic • **HEIGHT:** 4' 11" • **WEIGHT:** 238 lbs.
ATTACKS: Teleport, Confusion, Harden, Rapid Spin, Mud-Slap, Psybeam, Rock Tomb, Self-Destruct, Ancientpower, Sandstorm, Hyper Beam, Cosmic Power, Explosion

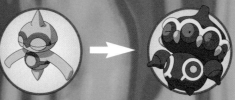

LILEEP Sea Lily Pokémon

TYPE: Rock/Grass • **HEIGHT:** 3' 3" • **WEIGHT:** 52 lbs.
ATTACKS: Astonish, Constrict, Acid, Ingrain, Confuse Ray, Amnesia, Ancientpower, Stockpile, Spit Up, Swallow

CRADILY Barnacle Pokémon

TYPE: Rock/Grass • **HEIGHT:** 4' 11" • **WEIGHT:** 133 lbs.
ATTACKS: Astonish, Constrict, Acid, Ingrain, Confuse Ray, Amnesia, Ancientpower, Stockpile, Spit Up, Swallow

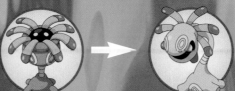

ANORITH
Old Shrimp Pokémon
TYPE: Rock/Bug
HEIGHT: 2' 4"
WEIGHT: 28 lbs.
ATTACKS: Scratch, Harden, Mud Sport, Water Gun, Metal Claw, Protect, Ancientpower, Fury Cutter, Slash, Rock Blast

ARMALDO
Plate Pokémon
TYPE: Rock/Bug
HEIGHT: 4' 11"
WEIGHT: 150 lbs.
ATTACKS: Scratch, Harden, Mud Sport, Water Gun, Metal Claw, Protect, Ancientpower, Fury Cutter, Slash, Rock Blast

FEEBAS
Fish Pokémon
TYPE: Water
HEIGHT: 2' 0"
WEIGHT: 16 lbs.
ATTACKS: Splash, Tackle, Flail

MILOTIC
Tender Pokémon
TYPE: Water
HEIGHT: 20' 4"
WEIGHT: 357 lbs.
ATTACKS: Water Fun, Wrap, Water Sport, Refresh, Water Pulse, Twister, Recover, Rain Dance, Hydro Pump, Attract, Safeguard

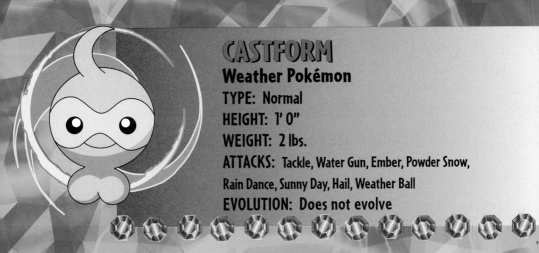

CASTFORM
Weather Pokémon
TYPE: Normal
HEIGHT: 1' 0"
WEIGHT: 2 lbs.
ATTACKS: Tackle, Water Gun, Ember, Powder Snow, Rain Dance, Sunny Day, Hail, Weather Ball
EVOLUTION: Does not evolve

KECLEON
Color Swap Pokémon
TYPE: Normal
HEIGHT: 3' 3"
WEIGHT: 49 lbs.
ATTACKS: Thief, Tail Whip, Astonish, Lick, Scratch, Bind, Faint Attack, Fury Swipes, Psybeam, Screech, Slash, Substitute, Ancientpower
EVOLUTION: Does not evolve

SHUPPET **Puppet Pokémon**

TYPE: Ghost • **HEIGHT:** 2' 0" • **WEIGHT:** 5 lbs.

ATTACKS: Knock Off, Screech, Night Shade, Cruise, Spite, Will-o-Wisp, Faint Attack, Shadow Ball, Snatch, Grudge

BANETTE **Marionette Pokémon**

TYPE: Ghost • **HEIGHT:** 3' 7" • **WEIGHT:** 28 lbs.

ATTACKS: Knock Off, Screech, Night Shade, Curse, Spite, Will-o-Wisp, Faint Attack, Shadow Ball, Snatch, Grudge

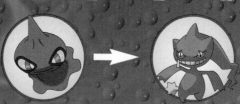

DUSKULL **Requiem Pokémon**

TYPE: Ghost • **HEIGHT:** 2' 7" • **WEIGHT:** 33 lbs.

ATTACKS: Leer, Night Shade, Disable, Foresight, Astonish, Confuse Ray, Pursuit, Curse, Will-o-Wisp, Mean Look, Future Sight

DUSCLOPS **Beckon Pokémon**

TYPE: Ghost • **HEIGHT:** 5' 3" • **WEIGHT:** 67 lbs.

ATTACKS: Bind, Leer, Night Shade, Disable, Foresight, Astonish, Confuse Ray, Pursuit, Curse, Shadow Punch, Will-o-Wisp, Mean Look, Future Sight

TROPIUS
Fruit Pokémon
TYPE: Grass/Flying
HEIGHT: 6' 7"
WEIGHT: 221 lbs.
ATTACKS: Leer, Gust, Growth, Razor Leaf, Stomp, Sweet Scent, Whirlwind, Magical Leaf, Body Slam, Solarbeam, Synthesis
EVOLUTION: Does not evolve

CHIMECHO
Wind Chime Pokémon
TYPE: Psychic
HEIGHT: 2' 0"
WEIGHT: 2 lbs.
ATTACKS: Wrap, Growl, Astonish, Confusion, Take Down, Uproar, Yawn, Psywave, Double-Edge, Heal Bell, Safeguard, Psychic
EVOLUTION: Does not evolve

ABSOL
Disaster Pokémon
TYPE: Dark
HEIGHT: 3' 11"
WEIGHT: 104 lbs.
ATTACKS: Scratch, Leer, Taunt, Quick Attack, Razor Wind, Bite, Swords Dance, Double-Team, Slash, Future Sight, Perish Song
EVOLUTION: Does not evolve

WYNAUT **Bright Pokémon**

TYPE: Psychic • HEIGHT: 2' • WEIGHT: 31 lbs.
ATTACKS: Splash, Charm, Encore, Counter, Mirror Coat, Safe Guard, Destiny Bond

SNORUNT
Snow Hat Pokémon
TYPE: Ice
HEIGHT: 2' 4"
WEIGHT: 37 lbs
ATTACKS: Powder Snow, Leer, Double-Team, Bite, Icy Wind, Headbutt, Protect, Crunch, Ice Beam, Hail, Blizzard

GLALIE
Face Pokémon
TYPE: Ice
HEIGHT: 4' 11"
WEIGHT: 566 lbs.
ATTACKS: Powder Snow, Leer, Double-Team, Bite, Icy Wind, Headbutt, Protect, Crunch, Ice Beam, Hail, Blizzard, Sheer Cold

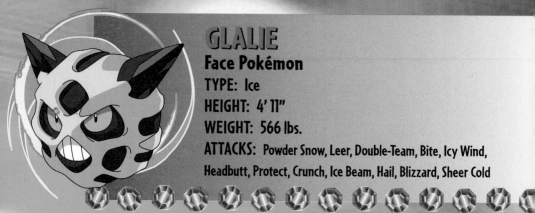

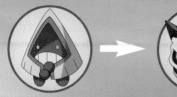

SPHEAL

Clap Pokémon
TYPE: Ice/Water
HEIGHT: 2' 7"
WEIGHT: 87 lbs.
ATTACKS: Powder Snow, Growl, Water Gun, Encore, Ice Ball, Body Slam, Aurora Beam, Hail, Rest, Snore, Blizzard, Sheer Cold

SEALEO

Ball Roll Pokémon
TYPE: Ice/Water
HEIGHT: 3' 7"
WEIGHT: 193 lbs.
ATTACKS: Powder Snow, Growl, Water Gun, Encore, Ice Ball, Body Slam, Aurora Beam, Hail, Rest, Snore, Blizzard, Sheer Cold

WALREIN

Ice Break Pokémon
TYPE: Ice/Water
HEIGHT: 4' 7"
WEIGHT: 332 lbs.
ATTACKS: Powder Snow, Growl, Water Gun, Encore, Ice Ball, Body Slam, Aurora Beam, Hail, Rest Snore, Blizzard, Sheer Cold

CLAMPERL
Bivalve Pokémon
TYPE: Water
HEIGHT: 1' 4"
WEIGHT: 116 lbs.
ATTACKS: Clamp, Water Gun, Whirlpool, Iron Defense

HUNTAIL
Deep Sea Pokémon
TYPE: Water
HEIGHT: 5' 7"
WEIGHT: 60 lbs.
ATTACKS: Whirlpool, Bite, Screech, Water Pulse, Scary Face,
Crunch, Baton Pass, Hydro Pump

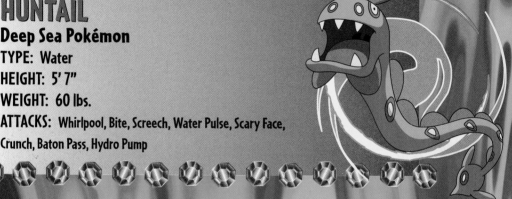

GOREBYSS
South Sea Pokémon
TYPE: Water
HEIGHT: 5' 11"
WEIGHT: 50 lbs.
ATTACKS: Whirlpool, Confusion, Agility, Water Pulse, Amnesia,
Psychic, Baton Pass, Hydro Pump

RELICANTH
Longevity Pokémon
TYPE: Water/Rock
HEIGHT: 3' 3"
WEIGHT: 52 lbs.
ATTACKS: Tackle, Harden, Water Gun, Rock Tomb, Yawn, Take Down, Mud Sport, Ancientpower, Rest, Double-Edge, Hydro Pump
EVOLUTION: Does not evolve

LUVDISC
Rendevous Pokémon
TYPE: Water
HEIGHT: 2' 0"
WEIGHT: 19 lbs.
ATTACKS: Tackle, Charm, Water Gun, Agility, Take Down, Attract, Sweet Kiss, Flail, Safeguard
EVOLUTION: Does not evolve

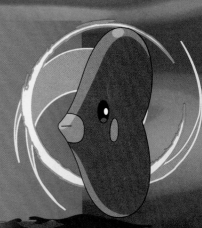

BAGON
Rock Head Pokémon
TYPE: Dragon
HEIGHT: 2' 0"
WEIGHT: 93 lbs.
ATTACKS: Rage, Bite, Leer, Headbutt, Focus Energy, Ember, Dragonbreath, Scary Face, Crunch, Dragon Claw, Double-Edge

SHELGON
Endurance Pokémon
TYPE: Dragon
HEIGHT: 3' 7"
WEIGHT: 244 lbs.
ATTACKS: Rage, Bite, Leer, Headbutt, Focus Energy, Ember, Protect, Dragonbreath, Scary Face, Crunch, Dragon Claw, Double-Edge

SALAMENCE
Blaze Pokémon
TYPE: Dragon
HEIGHT: 4' 11"
WEIGHT: 226 lbs.
ATTACKS: Rage, Bite, Leer, Headbutt, Focus Energy, Ember, Protect, Dragonbreath, Scary Face, Fly, Crunch, Dragon Claw, Double-Edge

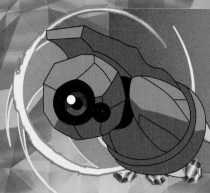

BELDUM
Iron Ball Pokémon
TYPE: Steel/Psychic
HEIGHT: 2' 0"
WEIGHT: 210 lbs.
ATTACKS: Take Down

MATANG
Iron Claw Pokémon
TYPE: Steel/Psychic
HEIGHT: 3' 11"
WEIGHT: 447 lbs.
ATTACKS: Take Down, Confusion, Metal Claw, Scary Face,
Pursuit, Psychic, Iron Defense, Meteor Mash, Agility, Hyper Beam

METAGROSS
Iron Leg Pokémon
TYPE: Steel/Psychic
HEIGHT: 5' 3"
WEIGHT: 1,213 lbs.
ATTACKS: Take Down, Confusion, Metal Claw, Scary Face,
Confusion, Pursuit, Psychic, Iron Defense, Meteor Mash,
Agility, Hyper Beam

REGIROCK
Rock Peak Pokémon
TYPE: Rock
HEIGHT: 5' 7"
WEIGHT: 507 lbs.
ATTACKS: Explosion, Rock Throw, Curse, Superpower, Ancientpower, Iron Defense, Amnesia, Zap Cannon, Lock-On, Hyper Beam
EVOLUTION: Does not evolve

REGICE
Iceberg Pokémon
TYPE: Ice
HEIGHT: 5' 11"
WEIGHT: 386 lbs.
ATTACKS: Explosion, Icy Wind, Curse, Superpower, Ancientpower, Amnesia, Zap Cannon, Lock-On, Hyper Beam
EVOLUTION: Does not evolve

REGISTEEL
Iron Pokémon
TYPE: Steel
HEIGHT: 6' 3"
WEIGHT: 452 lbs
ATTACKS: Explosion, Metal Claw, Curse, Superpower, Ancientpower, Iron Defense, Amnesia, Zap Cannon, Lock-On, Hyper Beam
EVOLUTION: Does not evolve

LATIAS

Eon Pokémon

TYPE: Dragon/Psychic

HEIGHT: 4' 7"

WEIGHT: 88 lbs.

ATTACKS: Psywave, Wish, Helping Hand, Safeguard, Water Sport, Refresh, Mist Ball, Psychic, Recover Charm

EVOLUTION: Does not evolve

LATIOS

Eon Pokémon

TYPE: Dragon/Psychic

HEIGHT: 6' 7"

WEIGHT: 132 lbs.

ATTACKS: Psywave, Memento, Helping Hand, Safeguard, Dragonbreath, Protect, Refresh, Luster, Purge

EVOLUTION: Does not evolve

KYOGRE
Sea Basin Pokémon
TYPE: Water
HEIGHT: 14' 9"
WEIGHT: 776 lbs.
ATTACKS: Water Pulse, Scary Face, Ancientpower, Body Slam, Calm Mind, Ice Beam, Hydro Pump, Rest, Sheer Cold, Double-Edge, Water Spout
EVOLUTION: Does not evolve

GROUDON
Continent Pokémon
TYPE: Ground
HEIGHT: 11' 6"
WEIGHT: 2,095 lbs.
ATTACKS: Mud Shot, Scary Face, Ancientpower, Slash, Bulk Up, Earthquake, Fire Blast, Rest, Fissure, Solar Beam, Eruption
EVOLUTION: Does not evolve

RAYQUAZA
Sky High Pokémon
TYPE: Dragon/Flying
HEIGHT: 23' 0"
WEIGHT: 455 lbs.
ATTACKS: Twister, Scary Face, Ancientpower, Dragon Claw, Dragon Dance, Crunch, Fly, Rest, Extremespeed, Outrage, Hyper Beam
EVOLUTION: Does not evolve